Butterfly Mandala Adult Color

60 Beautiful Butterfly Designs With Intricate Patterns For Stress Relief

By Omar Johnson

Get Your Free Mandala

Visit

ADULTCOLORINGBOOKSFORYOU.COM

Make Profits Easy LLC Publishing

profitsdaily123@aol.com

Copyright 2015